Out of Darkness and Into the Light
A Guide to Spiritual Wellness

Tracey Weeden

This book is dedicated to my daughter Tayla who has been a witness to "my gift". Let this guide inspire you and remind you of God's love. No matter what you may be faced with in this realm of life, He is with you.

God will always reveal His love. Be prepared. Be protected.

The purpose of this book is to convince you that God does exist and is very much alive. It is also meant to guide you through the process of building a stronger relationship with God. There is never a moment when He is not with us. His love and comfort is like the air that we breathe. If you look hard enough, you will see symbols from Heaven that are the signs of His love..

I believe that there are several layers to existence that I refer to as realms. Most Christians identify three: Earth, Heaven and Hell. However, I believe there is also a fourth realm...a spiritual realm that most humans tend to be oblivious to, overlook or escape from due to fear of the unknown. This realm co-exists with our earthly world. Within that realm, there too is life and death. While there is only one God, he does not always protect us from the pain caused by the Spirit realm or from the influence of evil caused by other humans because He expects us to shield ourselves with His armor against those forces. Angels also exist in the Spirit realm and act as direct messengers of God. They are used to protect us and to communicate with us; usually through our dreams or during states of complete oneness through meditation and stillness.

Much of how we view our purpose in the Earth-based realm of life is based upon our conscious experiences, lessons learned from those experiences (revelation) and from our reflection: the process when we examine how our experiences impact our lives. Our reflections often lead us to change. The changes that we make then begin to shape and mold us into who we become during our spiritual journey. Some experiences are in darkness and some experiences are in the light of this Earth-based realm and ultimately have a direct consequence on your view of the world and your purpose in life itself. Let us focus on the light.

The personal experiences that I describe in this guide seemed to occur during times when I was feeling that God was not with me. I may have been feeling overburdened, alone, detached from family and friends or significantly struggling with my faith in God. Despite my periods of feeling desolate, God managed to remind me both emotionally and symbolically that He was still by my side. As I experienced His symbols of faith, my faith grew stronger each time.

God has asked me to share my experiences, revelations and reflections with you so that you might better identify the signs of light from the Spirit world. I pray that this guide helps to prepare you as you take on or continue your journey in faith. Living in His light will lead you to do more of His work. This is my message to you who care to believe. I have proof. Take a look in love and light.

Experience:

He Came to Me; A Dream within a Dream

December 23, 2012

Around 8:00 pm I lay in bed since now my daughter was asleep and I anticipated time alone to reflect, unwind and prepare for another work day. During this time I worked as an administrator at a for-profit agency where every day brought new challenges. Due to the holiday season, I was under a lot of pressure to meet deadlines, which led to increased stress at work and unrest in my personal life as well.

On this night after a frustrating day and while feeling the demands of life, I started to feel like the weight of the world was on my shoulders, I decided to seek spiritual resolution since it seemed that nothing that I said or did seemed to help. My feelings of defeat naturally influenced my spiritual resolution and therefore did not come from a place of peace or forgiveness.

I scrolled frantically, yet carefully on the internet looking up Black Magic and Spells. My intentions were an attempt to control the negative environment around me through the power of old-fashioned witch craft. Although I was not experienced in this area, I was desperate. I stumbled upon a web-site based out of Africa, which through animal sacrifices, serpents and other unidentifiable substances, promised me the chance at power greater than I had ever known. The price was right too; only $49.99. Anyone who knows anything about the power of evil knows that the price was much greater than that.

Suddenly, I felt an overwhelming negative energy in my home. I jumped out of bed and turned to my lamp. I immediately noticed an ugly brown bug! The flat back, black spotted, 6-8 legged -bug with tentacles was slowly creeping up my bedroom wall! Its buzz was loud which startled me the most. I felt afraid. What had I done? The feeling of darkness was strong. I thought to myself, "Is my daughter okay?" But I couldn't move to check because I was frozen in fear.

I began to pray rapidly and precisely for God to protect my daughter and me from any harm. I prayed for forgiveness because I felt that I had betrayed Him. Why would He protect someone who so clearly betrayed Him?! I very well knew through years of Sunday school and growing up in a spiritual family that **all** power belongs to God! Why would I look elsewhere? Why couldn't I trust that He would make things better in His own time?

I found the courage to kill the "stink "bug with the closest shoe, removed my white sage from its satchel and continued to pray. I lit the sage, still praying, and waved it in the corner of every room. I prayed, "I rebuke all negative Spirits in the name of Jesus Christ of Nazareth. Our father who are in heaven hallowed be thy name, thy kingdom come, thy will be done, on earth as it is in heaven. Give us this day our daily bread and forgive us our trespasses as we forgive those who trespass against us and lead us not into temptation, but deliver us from evil, now and at the hour of our death. In the name of the Father, the Son and the Holy Spirit. Amen" The energy in my home felt less scary. I put out the fire on the sage, set my alarm and went to sleep.

I began to dream of being in a large white house with many levels. The grass outside was green and the yard was long. No other homes were visible. I pulled my truck into the garage, but somehow could not park straight. The garage was attached to the open living room of the house, so I had to park straight otherwise I would run over the couch. A friend of mine appeared and we began to argue about my inability to park straight. He escorted me out of the truck so that he could show me how to park it the right way. He then told me to go upstairs and lay down and go to sleep. When I fell asleep, I began to dream. I was experiencing a dream within a dream.

Two angels appeared to me. Each was very large and appeared long. Their wings were visible and their garbs were dark. I could not make out their facial features, yet I could see their expression which looked serious. I was so afraid! The Angels grabbed me by both of my arms with one on each side as if to ensure that I could not resist. A part of me very afraid, yet a part of me was also curious about where they were taking me. They guided me to a room. When we entered the room I was faced towards a blue empty wall. The angels moved to my left side just above my head, still looking very serious with flat expressions on their faces. They told me, "go into the light and stay away from darkness". I thought, "How could they know?" I was clearly exposed. My actions had not gone unnoticed.

My fear was overruled and suddenly I was filled with an amazing sense of peace. The peace was unlike any that I had ever experienced. No relaxation technique in this conscious realm could offer me the contentment that I felt within. At that point, nothing else mattered. It seemed like all of my life as I knew it on earth was erased. All of my fears were erased. All of my stress was erased. I could see my daughter sleeping in bed and knew that I was leaving her behind, but that too did not matter. I could not help feeling that I was in paradise, cleansed and released from all of my human inhibitions. My soul was completely free.

In my right ear, I heard a voice. It was not male or female, nor adult or child. It was direct and firm, yet loving and protective. The voice said, "Go into the light and do more of my work. Go into the light and do more of my work. Go into the light and do more of my work". The message was delivered in a clear, steady powerful tone. I knew that this was the voice of God talking to me. The feelings of joy and protection intensified. I wanted to stay and listen forever. I had so many questions. My mind began racing. He had chosen me! He had come to me! He had saved me! So imperfect me! So disobedient me! Why me? He finally told me in a much more nurturing voice, "You cannot stay". I turned to the angels who seemed to now look pitiful towards me. One of the angels said, "Return to your dream". I became eager to have some questions answered before I had to leave. The first question was in reference to companionship in my conscious realm of life. They looked at me more pitifully. It appeared that one Angel wanted to answer, but could not. Then the Angel said, "Return to your dream."

I returned to my first dream and awoke. Something told me that it is time to wake up and write this down.

Revelation: One Hundred Seven Days Later

I was moved to a new career that consisted of helping a larger geographical area and much more diverse group of individuals. The work load was heavier. The needs of the individuals served, my peers, staff and the community at large were not only physiologically intense, but spiritually intense as well. I soon realized that such type of work felt much more fulfilling as it allowed me to practice my spiritual depth of understanding in this Earth-based realm of life. This job seemed to test every spiritual conviction that I believed in. It empowered me to use my voice to advocate for change and fairness for populations who voice often times went unheard. It also empowered me to use my heart, which felt overwhelming filled with joy as the services to the community were improved. There was no doubt in my mind that I had begun the journey of fulfilling God's purpose for my life.

Reflection

The experience of hearing from God has changed my life. It has forced me to seek Him in everything I do. Of course there are those times when I feel overwhelmed and I allow the darkness of this world get me down. Yet, unlike before this experience, I have learned that the only way out of that darkness is through prayer and trust in God. *All* things are truly possible through Him. There is nothing in this Earth-based realm of life that is more important to me than knowing that I am here to do His will.

I have learned through my dreams that as humans, it is not each other that we need to worry about and avoid, but it is the evil forces of darkness that exist in the Spirit world. As the bible states, "For our struggle is not against flesh and blood, but against the ruler, against the authorities, against the powers of this dark world and against the spiritual forces of evil in the heavenly realms." (Ephesians 6:12 NIV)

Reading this passage means so much more to me now than it did years before. Living in a world of light and darkness does not always make it easy to distinguish between what is real and what is not real. Our society shapes us to fit into the mold that has been created for us; a mold that is bias, prejudice, selective and unloving most of the time.

In the past, I would at times feel that I was literally fighting against the forces of darkness. These forces may have appeared as a desire for an abundance of money, a larger home, a newer car, harder soled shoes, brighter jewelry and everything else that was tangible. I now realize that dependence on those worldly items is not what God expects of me. Those items are not vital necessities when living in the light of this realm. In the realm of light, none of those objects matter. They will not justify my right into passage through the gates of Heaven. In the Earth-based realm, they simply provide a level of access to more objects and in some cases provide a showcase of status; neither of which mean anything when you meet God. God wants us to know that he truly provides us with everything that we need. He provides us with love, protection, wisdom, fairness, patience and a promise that we will be with Him in everlasting life.

As I continue along my spiritual journey, God has so generously provided me with seemingly random reminders that He is with me; the realm of realm of the Spirit World is always with me. Thus, I feel led to share my reminders with you so that in faith, you too can know that God loves you and is watching over you even when you feel like the least deserving of His grace and mercy.

God be with you now and always.

Experience

Revelation

Reflection

Experience: Taken at Haven United Methodist Church (2008). This picture was taken during Children's Sunday celebration. The picture is of one of the children reading scripture at the pulpit. The light of the pulpit transformed to a Dove. There were no visible birds in the church.

Revelation: When all the people were being baptized, Jesus was baptized too. And as he was praying heaven was opened and the Holy Spirit descended on him in bodily form like a dove. And a voice came from heaven, "You are my Son, whom I love, with you I am well pleased." (Luke 3:21-22 NIV)

Reflection: God sends us his Dove of life as a reminder that indeed He lives. It is a symbol of faith and a reason to celebrate the realm of this life that he has given to you. The Dove of Life represents God's love and everlasting peace.

When have you experienced the Dove of Life? Where were you? Who were you with? How were you feeling?

_____
_____
_____
_____
_____
_____
_____

How does the Dove of Life speak to you?

_____
_____
_____
_____
_____
_____
_____

What has the Dove of Life revealed to you since your encounter with it?

_____
_____
_____
_____
_____
_____
_____

Experience: Taken at Camp Hoover (2014).

Revelation: The Lord is my shepherd. I shall not be in want. He makes me lie down in green pastures, he leads me beside quiet waters, He restores my soul. (Psalm 23:1-3 NIV)

Reflection: The Spirit of God is all around you. At your lowest points, he provides comfort, rest and assurance through his beautiful masterpiece. He has created a realm of this world in the like of his Kingdom in Heaven where every soul can find Him waiting with open arms.

When have you experienced being in the calming presence of water? Where were you? Who were you with? How were you feeling?

_____
_____
_____
_____
_____
_____
_____

How does the quietness of this lake speak to you?

_____
_____
_____
_____
_____
_____
_____

What has your experience near water revealed to you?

_____
_____
_____
_____
_____
_____
_____

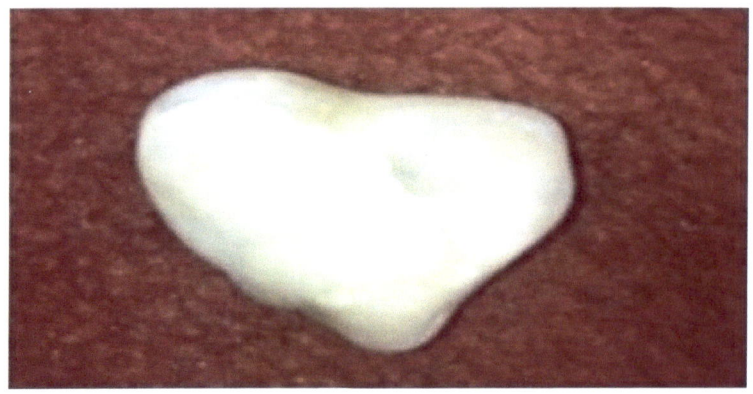

Experience: This is a rock that I stumbled upon at Horseneck Beach (2014) while visiting my mother who was very ill and hospitalized. This was a very emotional time of my life.

Revelation: My soul finds rest in God alone; my salvation comes from him. He alone is my rock and my salvation; he is my fortress, I will never be shaken. (Psalm 62:1-2 NIV)

Reflection: The love of God comes at times when you least expect it. It may also come in form when you are not seeking it. His love is freeing and omnipresent. Later research on heart rocks revealed that this particular rock is a sign of comfort.

When have you either bought or found an object in shape of a heart? What attracted you to it? How did it make you feel?

_____
_____
_____
_____
_____
_____
_____

How does this heart rock speak to you?

_____
_____
_____
_____
_____
_____
_____

How will you let God shape his love for you?

_____
_____
_____
_____
_____
_____
_____

Experience: Echo Lake Park (2011). These branches have created a bind that has stayed strong despite the strong winds, hurricanes and snow storms that have knocked down much stronger looking branches and trees around it.

Revelation: My son, keep your father's commands and do not forsake you mother's teaching. Bind them upon your heart forever; fasten them around your neck. When you walk, they will guide you; when you sleep, they will watch over you; when you awake, they will speak to you. (Proverbs 7:20-22 NIV)

Reflection: Our Father has given me the information and tools to do His will. Whenever I feel stuck or are in search of answers, I go to His Book. He has provided me with the answers to untwist the entanglements in my life.

Has there ever been a time when you felt bound to someone or something that interfered with your ability to love God?

_____
_____
_____
_____
_____
_____
_____

How did you free yourself from that feeling of being bound or entangled?

_____
_____
_____
_____
_____
_____
_____

How will you continue to let God set you free from the turmoil of entanglements?

_____
_____
_____
_____
_____
_____
_____

Experience: This picture was taken in New Jersey (2014) as I backed out of my driveway. I was feeling down, lonely and in a rush to find some way to fill my time. I could not believe my eyes! I took the first picture quickly in case the symbol disappeared and then I backed out for a closer shot. I tried to identify where this "reflection" was coming form, but I could not find the source.

Revelation: I have great confidence in you; I take great pride in you. I am greatly encouraged; in all our troubles my joy knows no bounds. (2 Corinthians 7:4 NIV)

Reflection: God appears in your life when you least expect Him. Take the time to see what He may be showing you.

When have you discovered symbols that were unexpected, yet meaningful to you? What type of symbol was it? How did it make you feel?

_____
_____
_____
_____
_____
_____
_____

How does this symbol speak to you?

_____
_____
_____
_____
_____
_____
_____

How will you interpret the symbols that God reveals to you?

_____
_____
_____
_____
_____
_____
_____

Experience: Orlando, Florida (2009). During my first visit to Florida I woke up early to catch the sunrise. I snapped the picture while embracing my new surroundings and this is what I received.

Revelation: And anyone who does not take his cross and follow me is not worthy of me. (Mathew 10:38 NIV)

Reflection: The most precious symbol in Christianity is the cross. The cross is a reminder to you that Jesus, the Son of God, died for your sins so that you would not suffer as He did. The beauty of the glowing rays leads you to the light of God and to the splendor of his majesty.

Think about a time when you have encountered the burden of a cross. How did it make you feel?

_____
_____
_____
_____
_____
_____
_____

How does this cross speak to you?

_____
_____
_____
_____
_____
_____
_____

What do you need from God during times when you feel that your cross is more that you can bear?

_____
_____
_____
_____
_____
_____
_____

Experience: High Point, New Jersey (2013). It was a dreary winter day. The leaves on the trees were at rest, the area was mostly empty of visitors and the only interesting objects to photograph seemed to be the clouds. This cloud looks like an Angel sounding a trumpet.

Revelation: Then the seven angels who had the seven trumpets prepared to sound them. (Revelations 8:6 NIV)

Reflection: The time is near that the seven angels will sound their trumpets and a third of the earth will be killed. Living as a child of God is more that saying, "I believe". It is requires preparation for the day that God will come and enter you into his kingdom of eternal life. This realm of life was created as a test meant to prepare you for the days to come.

Have you ever thought about where you will be when the Angels sound their trumpets? What do you imagine your life will be like?

_____
_____
_____
_____
_____
_____
_____

How does this picture speak to you?

_____
_____
_____
_____
_____
_____
_____

How will you prepare for a new life with God?

_____
_____
_____
_____
_____
_____
_____

Experience: High Point, New Jersey (2013). This photo speaks for itself.

Revelation: Open up, O heavens, and pour out your righteousness. Let the earth open wide so salvation and righteousness can sprout up together. I, the Lord, created them. (Isaiah 45:8 NIV)

Reflection: The superficial objects and false gods of this world can seem very appealing. It may lead you to sacrificing your overall well-being so that you can fill your life with stuff. God asks that you remove that stuff and reclaim the gifts that can be found in Him. There is no cost for living a life according to God, but the rewards are infinite.

Think about a time when it appeared that the sky had opened up just for you? How did this make you feel?

_____
_____
_____
_____
_____
_____

How do the vibrancies of the sun speak to you?

_____
_____
_____
_____
_____
_____

What "stuff" prevents you from opening the clouds of God into your life?

_____
_____
_____
_____
_____
_____

Experience: New Jersey (2013) While getting into the car we noticed a heart on the ground during a crisp autumn morning.

Revelation: I declare to you, brothers, that flesh and blood cannot inherit the kingdom of God, nor does the perishable inherit the imperishable. Listen, I tell you a mystery: We will not all sleep, but we will all be changed. (1 Corinthians 15:50-51 NIV)

Reflection: Change is not easy. As humans in this realm of life, we have the tendency to become accustomed to our surroundings. You may rely on routines and familiarity of the people and places around you to bring you through to another day. God has asked that you not get comfortable in your routines and to stay alert for opportunities to do more of His work.

Is there a particular season when you feel ready to make adjustments in your life? What season is it?

_____
_____
_____
_____
_____
_____
_____

What do you feel that God is asking you to change?

_____
_____
_____
_____
_____
_____
_____

How can you begin to prepare yourself for change?

_____
_____
_____
_____
_____
_____
_____

Experience: At my home in New Jersey (2014). This year was one of the worst winters that I can recall. It seemed like it would never end. Snow covered streets made leaving the house difficult and the days grew dark fast. I opened my blind hoping for a glimpse of sunshine. When I looked up I saw this stick figured cross wedged between my window and the snow.

Revelation: Be joyful in hope, patient in affliction, and faithful in prayer. (Romans 12:12 NIV)

Reflection: Even when there seems like no way out, no light in the mist of darkness; He is with you.

How has God shown you mercy and offered you hope?

What more do you need from God to feel His love and presence?

How have you thanked Him?

Experience: Traffic, New Jersey (2013). I was on my way home and there was an unusual amount of traffic. I remember feeling impatient. Looking out into the sky changed my focus.

Revelations: By day the Lord went ahead of them in a pillar of cloud to guide them on their way and by night in a pillar of fire to give them light, so that they could travel by day or night. (Exodus 13:21 NIV)

Reflection: God wants you to allow Him to be your light out of darkness.

Has there ever been a time when light seemed to appear even when your surroundings seemed very dark? Where was the light coming from?

_____
_____
_____
_____
_____
_____
_____

How did this light affect your mood or thoughts?

_____
_____
_____
_____
_____
_____
_____

During times of darkness where can you look to find this light again?

_____
_____
_____
_____
_____
_____
_____

Experience: The Great Swamp, New Jersey (2014).

Revelation: Trust in the Lord with all your heart and lean not on your own understanding; in all your ways acknowledge him, and he will make your paths straight. (Proverbs 3:5 NIV)

Reflection: As you continue on this journey through life, know that God is with you. You will have to decide which path to choose; the path leading to light or the path leading to darkness.

Where are you on the path of your spiritual journey?

_____
_____
_____
_____
_____
_____
_____

What keeps you on your path and what defers you from your path?

_____
_____
_____
_____
_____
_____
_____

What can you do to remain on a path lit with the light of God?

_____
_____
_____
_____
_____
_____
_____

Opportunities to Feel *Closer* to God

Experience: (where were you, how were you feeling at that time, what did you need)

_____
_____
_____
_____
_____
_____
_____

Revelation: (what does the Scripture say about your experience)

_____
_____
_____
_____
_____
_____
_____

How were you changed? (what was the outcome of your experience, did it bring you closer to God)

_____
_____
_____
_____
_____
_____
_____

Affix a picture of your experience here:

Experience: (where were you, how were you feeling at that time, what did you need)

_____
_____
_____
_____
_____

Revelation: (what does the Scripture say about your experience)

_____
_____
_____
_____
_____

How were you changed? (what was the outcome of your experience, did it bring you closer to God)

_____
_____
_____
_____
_____

Out of Darkness and Into the Light

Affix a picture of your experience here:

Experience: (where were you, how were you feeling at that time, what did you need)

_____
_____
_____
_____
_____

Revelation: (what does the Scripture say about your experience)

_____
_____
_____
_____
_____

How were you changed? (what was the outcome of your experience, did it bring you closer to God)

_____
_____
_____
_____
_____

Affix a picture of your experience here:

Experience: (where were you, how were you feeling at that time, what did you need)

_____
_____
_____
_____
_____

Revelation: (what does the Scripture say about your experience)

_____
_____
_____
_____
_____

How were you changed? (What was the outcome of your experience, did it bring you closer to God)

_____
_____
_____
_____
_____

www.ingramcontent.com/pod-product-compliance
Lightning Source LLC
Chambersburg PA
CBHW041743040426
42444CB00001B/1